The Adventures of Scuba Jack
Copyright 2022 by Beth Costanzo
All rights reserved

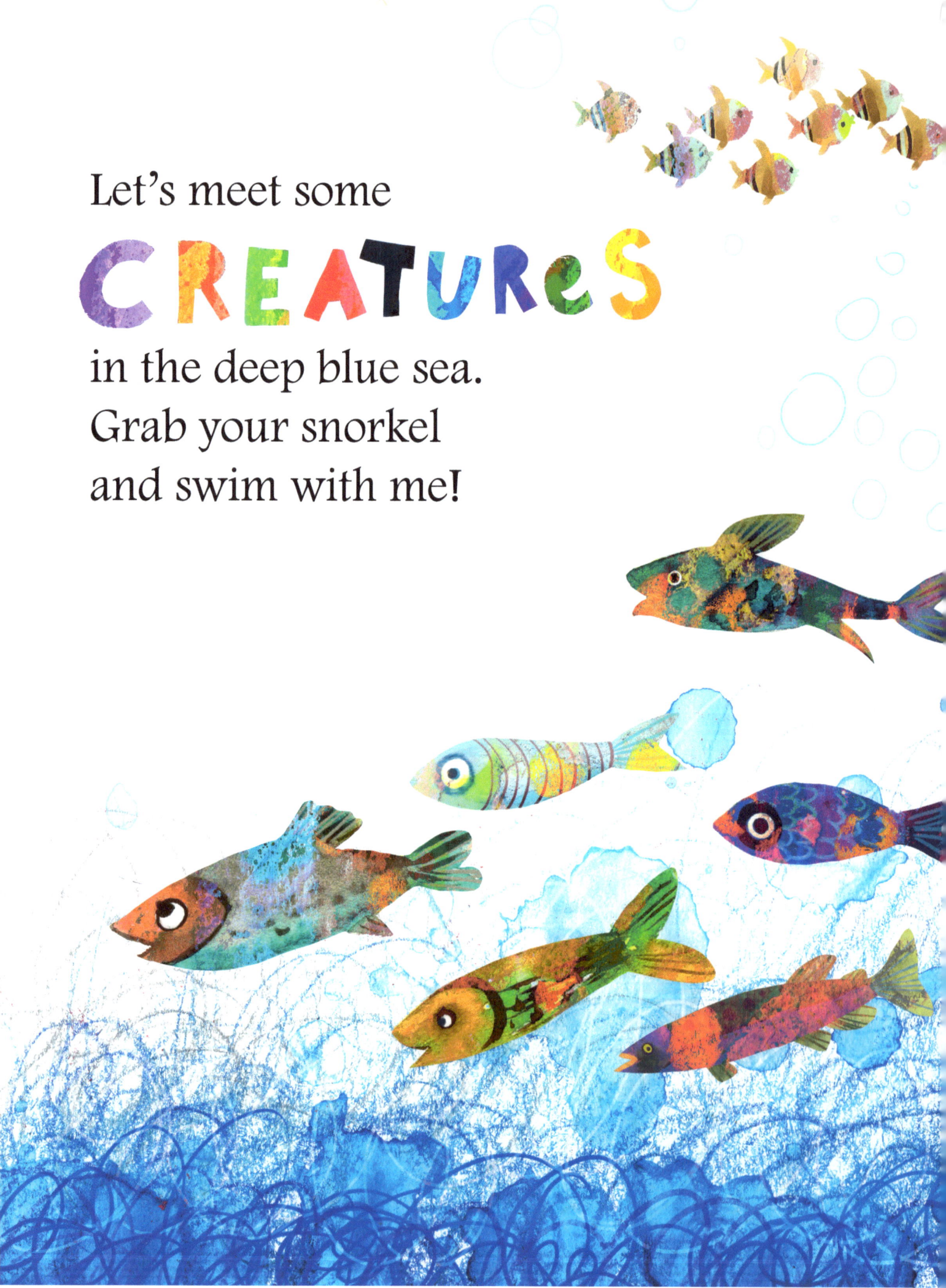

Let's meet some CREATURES in the deep blue sea. Grab your snorkel and swim with me!

Scuba Jack explores shipwrecks on the ocean floor. **HAMMER HEAD SHARKS** swim close to the shore.

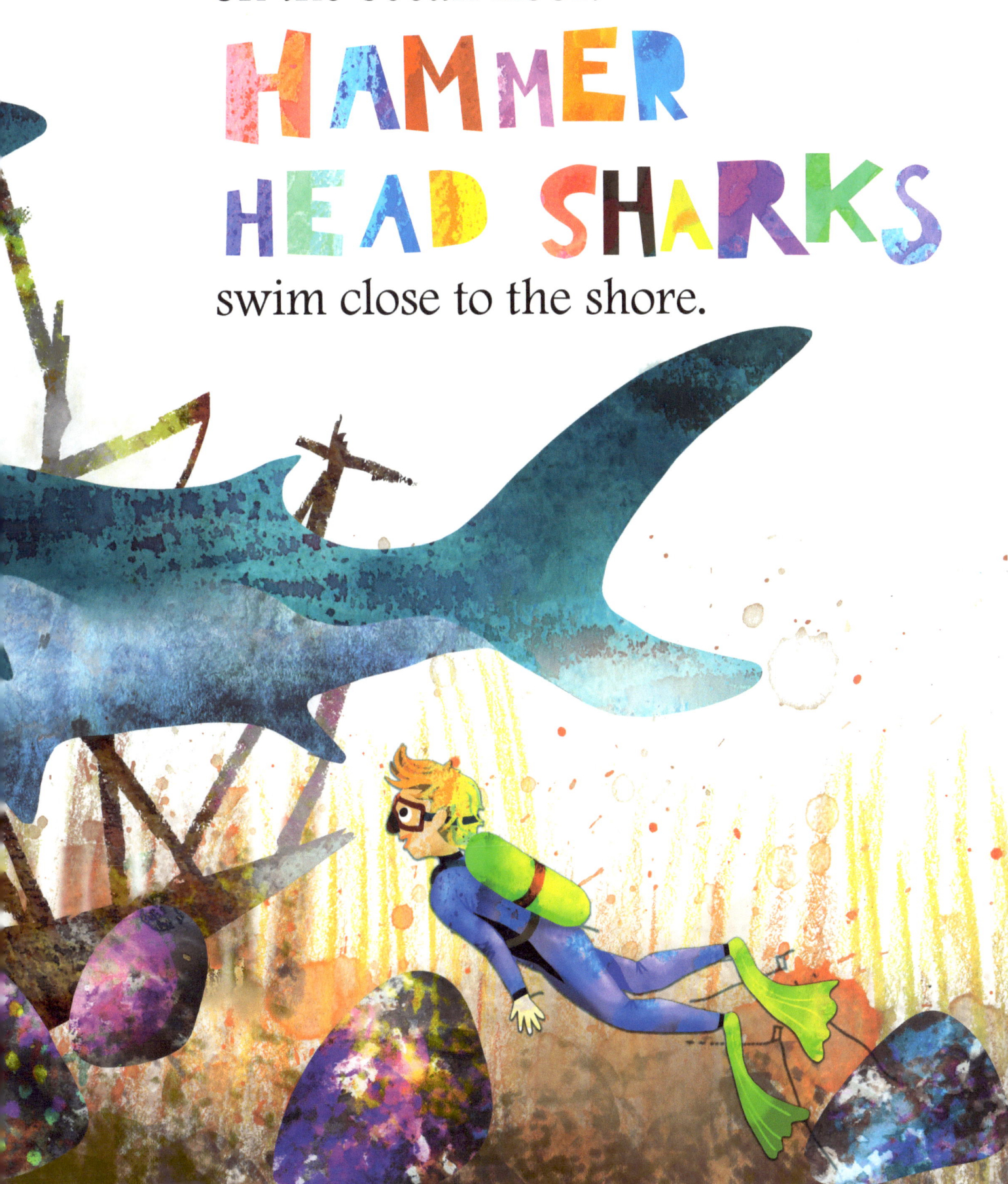

BLUE WHALES

think that they can fly.
They leap out of the water
and touch the sky.

Now we are deep and far below.
THE LANTERN FISH
are all aglow.

THE HUMPBACK WHALE

swims quickly along.
This beautiful creature
sings a magical song.

SEA TURTLES

make a nest on land.
They lay their eggs in the warm,
soft sand.

SEA URCHINS

are a Sea Otter's favorite snack.
He cracks them open,
while floating on his back.

Is that a tiny shock you feel?
Then you just met an
ELECTRIC EEL

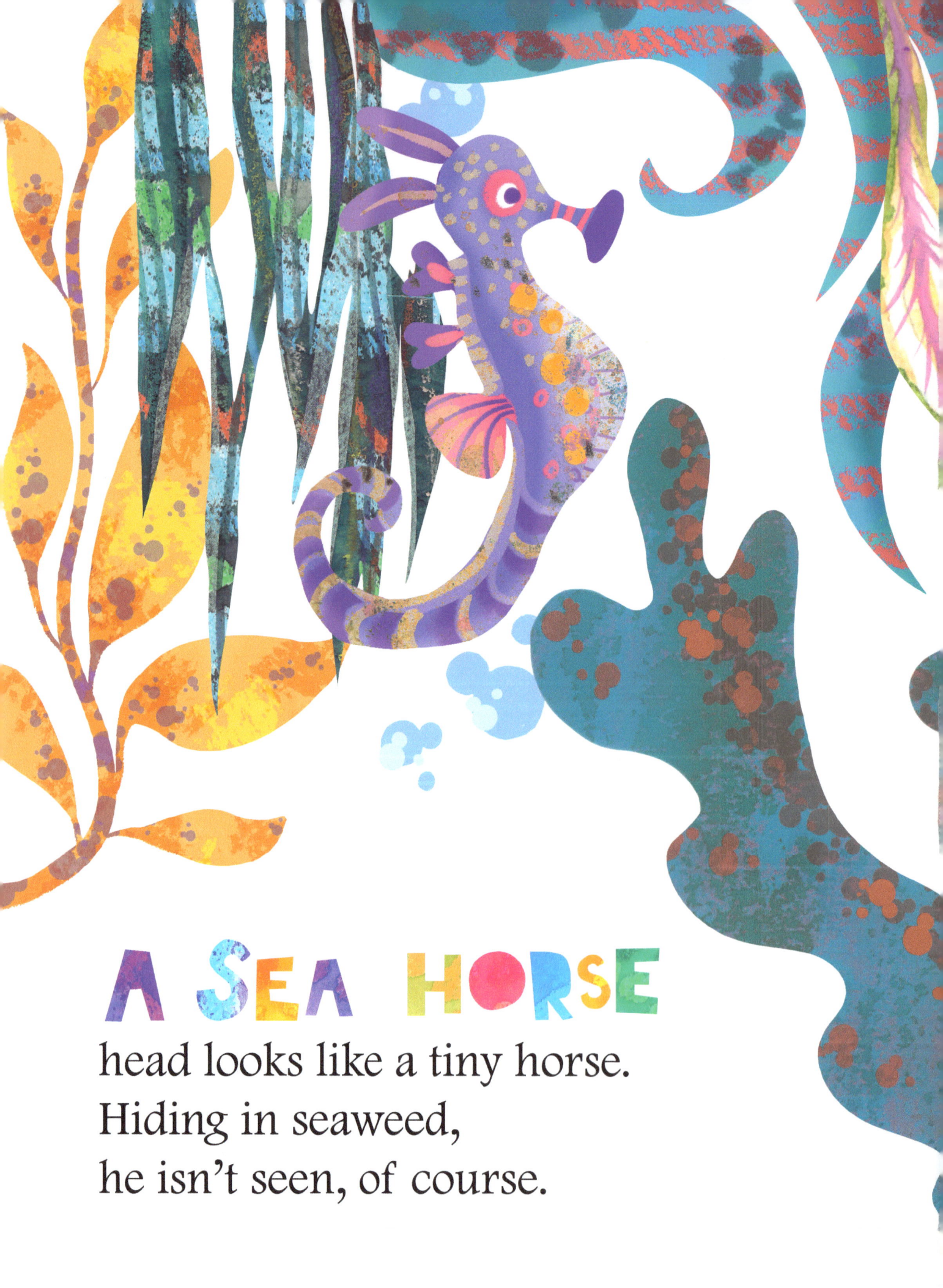

A SEA HORSE
head looks like a tiny horse.
Hiding in seaweed,
he isn't seen, of course.

Look, the BOTTLENOSE DOLPHINS came to hunt and play.
Echolocation is how he finds its prey.

A JELLY FISH

has tentacles and jiggles like jelly in the sea.
He shoots out water and swims past me!

We met some amazing creatures in the deep blue sea! Thanks for coming on this **AMAZING** adventure with me!